Quiet Mysteries

Glimpses of Shropshire

by *Gordon Dickins*

Shropshire Books

Front cover: Sunrise from Lyth Hill.

Back Cover: Near Berrington.

© Gordon Dickins 1995.

ISBN: 0-903802-67-8.

Cover and book design: Paul Brasenell.
Managing Editor: Helen Sample.
Published by Shropshire Books,
the publishing imprint of Shropshire County Council's
Information and Community Services Department.

Printed in Great Britain by Precision Colour Printing, Telford.

Dedicated to my father

Acknowledgements

I should like to thank Hawkstone Park Leisure Ltd. for permission to reproduce photographs taken in Hawkstone Park and Mr. and Mrs.P.Trevor-Jones for allowing me to include shots of their beautiful gardens at Preen Manor. Thanks also to Mrs.D.Davies and Miss M.Davies of Mamble near Kidderminster.

In the course of taking the photographs I have met many people who have suggested new locations or offered those snippets of local knowledge which are so valuable. Thanks to them all. And to many others who have attended talks or slide show presentations that I have given over the years and, through their comments and suggestions, indirectly contributed to this book. In particular I should like to thank all the parishioners of Hope and Worthen who made me so welcome for my talk at Worthen village hall last March. Finally, thanks to friends and colleagues within Shropshire County Council's Information and Community Services Department and members of the Mary Webb Society for their interest and support.

Helen Sample, Editor of Shropshire Books, has given me help and encouragement throughout the project as well as sorting out my grammatical mistakes while Paul Brasenell's professional design skills and Kathryn Green's illustrations have tranformed my basic text and photographs.

Thanks to Julie, once again, for her support and patience over the last two years while I have been working on Quiet Mysteries.

The publishers would like to thank the copyright holders (or their representatives) for permission to print extracts from the following works: *"Howard's End"*, E. M. Forster, *"A Shropshire Lad"*, A. E. Housman, *"Green Rain"*, *"House In Dormer Forest"*, *"The Golden Arrow"*, Mary Webb, *"St. Mawr"*, D. H. Lawrence, *"The Old Stone House"*, Walter de la Mare, *"English Hours"*, Henry James.

Technical Details

*A*ll the photographs, bar one, were taken on a 35mm, Nikon FM2 camera with 24mm., 28-70mm. and 70-210mm lenses using Fuji slide film. The one odd shot was taken on an ancient Voightlander compact, bought for £7.50 at a junk shop! About two thirds of the shots were taken with the aid of a tripod.

About the Author

Gordon Dickins was brought up in the Shropshire village of Coalport and attended schools in Madeley and Coalbrookdale before taking a degree in English at Bangor University. After working as a library assistant with Shropshire County Library he completed a post-graduate diploma in librarianship at Manchester Polytechnic. Returning to Shropshire he worked in libraries in Shrewsbury, Market Drayton and Wellington. Since 1980 he has specialised in children's work and is currently head of Children's and Schools' library services within Shropshire County Council's Information & Community Services Department.

Gordon has been involved in photography for seventeen years, landscape being his favourite subject. A parallel interest is the literary history of Shropshire and he is the author of *Shropshire Seasons*, *An Illustrated Literary Guide to Shropshire* and co-author of *Walks With Writers*. He has contributed to Radio Shropshire and Radio 4 programmes on Shropshire writers and to the Channel 4 television series Literary Island. He is vice-President of the Mary Webb Society. Gordon lives in Shrewsbury and spends much of his spare time in the Shropshire countryside, walking, taking photographs and enjoying his favourite landscape.

Introduction

"Quiet mysteries were in progress behind those tossing horizons: the West, as ever, was retreating with some secret which may not be worth the discovery, but which no practical man will ever discover."

(E.M. Forster: Howard's End, Ch. XXV)

Whenever I read these words I think how perceptive Forster was in identifying at least part of what makes Shropshire so special. In *Howard's End* the Shropshire hills around the fictional village of Oniton (Clun) are symbolic of the romantic west, beyond which the sun unfailingly sets. The fact that Shropshire is a border county bestows a further layer of romance and mystery to add to its overall mystique. Throughout history, throughout literature, the search for what lies beyond the western horizon has proved inspirational. I am sure that few of us can resist the attraction of a glorious sunset or the seemingly endless afterglow on a clear summer's evening. I spent a memorable evening in the hills above Clun photographing the sun as it set, a fiery globe, below the horizon, suddenly aware that a heavy, full moon was rising in the eastern sky behind me. That whole interminable continuum of night and day, east and west, was never more apparent.

A.E. Housman and D.H. Lawrence also touched on some of the quintessential aspects of Shropshire. Housman, with his bitter-sweet nostalgia, his emotive conjuring of an idyllic landscape - something seen, experienced, recalled in the mind's eye, but which can never be regained:

Into my heart an air that kills
From yon far country blows:
What are those blue remembered hills,
What spires, what farms are those?

That is the land of lost content,
I see it shining plain,
The happy highways where I went
And cannot come again.

(A Shropshire Lad, XL)

Lawrence, the third of these visitors from outside Shropshire, sensed the primeval nature of the landscape, the very age and immovability of what lies beneath the surface, somehow foreboding. Here, the Devil's Chair on the Stiperstones:

*"They came at last, trotting in file along a narrow track between heather, along the saddle of
a hill, to where the knot of pale granite suddenly cropped out. It was one of those places
where the spirit of aboriginal England still lingers, the old savage England, whose last blood
flows still in a few Englishmen, Welshmen, Cornishmen."*

(From St.Mawr)

All three writers touch on some of Shropshire's inner truths. None alone gives a satisfactory analysis of what Shropshire is and, thank goodness, it is unlikely that anyone ever will be able to define such an elusive concept. The very elusiveness, the half-sensed elements which defy analysis are what make Shropshire special. Perhaps the nearest anyone has ever come to succeeding in this is Mary Webb. Read one of her novels, or some of her poems, and share the imaginative responses of this Shropshire-born writer. Few have written so fervently, so sensitively or with such integrity about their own landscape.

To refer to the Shropshire landscape is misleading; it is made up of many landscapes and the variety of its scenery has often been commented on. In photographing the county I have come to the realisation that this scenery does not exist in isolation, did not evolve in isolation - it has all been moulded in some way by human activity, century after century. Perhaps I am stating the obvious here but one thing about photography is that it does make you look more closely at what is around you. I have begun to see just how people have changed the land, and in doing so, have sensed the echoes, the ghosts if you like, of those who have gone before. You have only to look around Shropshire to see the origins of those echoes; from Bronze Age remains such as Mitchell's Fold, Iron Age hillforts, deserted medieval villages and so on. The whole spectrum of recorded history is represented within the county right up to those still poignant echoes from the last war, deserted airfields, derelict hangars, servicemen's graves in country churchyards.

In creating this book I have tried to capture something of the intangible, knowing full well that it is an impossibility, tried to interpret some of those "quiet mysteries" which Forster referred to, remembering always that, wherever we are, we are always beyond someone else's horizon. So I have photographed Shropshire from sunrise to sunset, generally from east to west but with a few diversions en route. Some of the subjects are well known others less so but just as characteristic, perhaps even more so. I have not covered every part of the county and am very much aware that I have missed just as many attractive locations as I have included. Those I have omitted will be treats in store for me on future occasions.

I am not the first person to say that however well you know Shropshire you will always discover new places to visit or realise that there are different ways to view familiar ones. You will also make connections of which you were previously unaware. I firmly believe that much of the pleasure of reading, or enjoying music or art comes from those uniquely individual connections which we all make. We not only read or listen or look but bring something of ourselves to the piece in question. Looking at a beautiful landscape is just the same for me - it may be beautiful in its own right but it triggers off other images, other thoughts which go beyond the purely visual.

I can only offer you visual images here but I hope you may be prompted to go out and discover the potential of the infinite mysteries which Shropshire has to offer.

Gordon Dickins
August 1995

x

Sunrise

*H*ow bloodily the sun begins to peer
Above yon busky hill!
The day looks pale
At his distemperature.

(William Shakespeare: *King Henry IV, Part 1; Act V, Scene 1*)

Sunrise

Stretton Hills

After three unsuccessful attempts to photograph the sunrise from the Stretton Hills,
due to thick cloud, I finally managed to get myself to the right place at the right time
and with a clear sky above me. The sunrise was marvellous and I am left with images,
both mental and photographic, which are as vivid to me now as they were at the time.
One of nature's "quiet mysteries" unfolded before me as the faintest hint of light in the east
gradually became an all-enveloping, subtly changing flood of yellows and pinks,
the scene below emerging from darkness, at one with the sky.

From Caer Caradoc

*F*irst light on an August morning, looking from Caradoc towards the hills of the Welsh border.
The long white line in the middle distance is low-lying mist following
the course of the River Severn.

The Lawley and the Wrekin

Quarter past five in the morning and I parked below Caradoc, walked quietly past a solitary house and turned into the woods behind. Immediately the peace was disturbed by a tremendous flapping and cawing as every rook in the vicinity decided to panic. Feeling somewhat guilty as the cause of all this noise I emerged onto the hillside, looked back and saw the tops of the two hills silhouetted against the spreading light.

Towards Brown Clee

*A*s the sun rose a vivid, pinkish light bathed the scene, highlighting every eastern facing slope. In the far distance Brown Clee, Shropshire's highest hill, stands beyond Wenlock Edge and Corvedale.

Church Stretton and the Long Mynd

*T*he view south, looking down the length of the Long Mynd as the first sunlight transforms the scene.

The Wrekin

*T*he changing hues and tones of a summer sunrise, the Wrekin now pale mauve against a yellow-orange sky.

Towards Wenlock Edge

*T*he subtle tones of first light rapidly change to brilliance as the sun rises in the sky.
Wenlock Edge, that long, distinctive limestone escarpment, seems almost to glow,
too dazzling to look at for more than a few moments.

Winter sunrise, Edgmond

A translucent sky reflected in waterlogged tractor ruts in a field near Edgmond
where street lights are pin-pricks of light, like glow-worms.

Lilleshall Monument

*T*he flat lands of the Weald Moors end with the rocky outcrop at Lilleshall. The village lies below and beyond the hill which is topped by this 70 foot obelisk in memory of George Leveson-Gower, the first Duke of Sutherland who died in 1833. He was responsible for a massive programme of road building in Scotland but Lilleshall Hall was one of his homes and his estate in Shropshire was extensive. Lilleshall Hall is now the National Sports Centre.

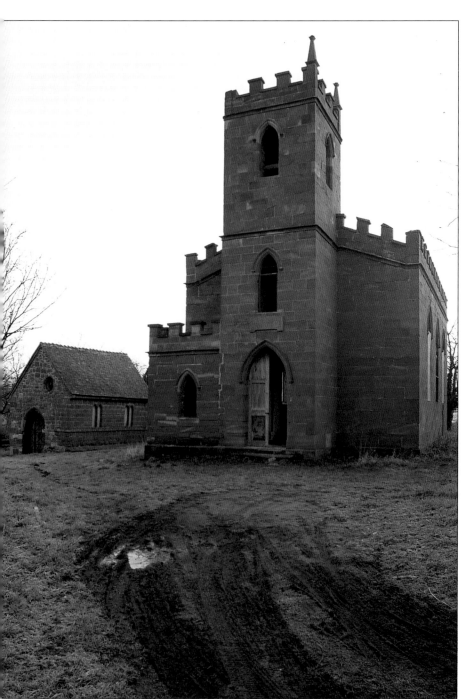

Longford, near Newport

St. Mary's church of 1806, with pink stone exaggerated
by the early morning light, stands derelict and slightly
forbidding. Beyond it is the preserved chancel of
an earlier church containing a late seventeenth
century monument to Thomas Talbot.

The Wrekin from the Long Mynd

*S*unrise on a freezing morning in March and a view from the lower slopes of the Long Mynd above All Stretton.
The lights in the bottom right hand corner of the picture are from one of those welcome respites
for the weary traveller offering breakfast, tea and toilets.

River Tern, Attingham

*M*ist still hangs over the Tern, close to its confluence with the Severn. Soon the warm spring sun will burn off the last traces - shape and form, tone and texture will be revealed but the day's magic will have passed.

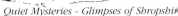

Ironbridge Gorge

*D*awn on a chilly September morning,
looking downstream from the bridge towards
Jackfield and Coalport.

River Severn, Ironbridge

*L*ooking upstream now from the Iron Bridge; the sun has
just risen and its rays are catching the tops of the trees
below Benthall Edge. It is hard to believe that the Severn
Valley Railway ran, until just over thirty years ago, through
the now-dense trees. Also buried here beneath moss,
brambles and foliage, are remnants of our industrial past -
limestone quarries and kilns, mining detritus and other
reminders that the industrial activity of the eighteenth and
nineteenth centuries extended to both banks of the river.

The Iron Bridge

A beautiful structure which, in my childhood
and those of generations before me, was primarily
a functional piece of engineering. Now it is a shrine, a symbol
of the Industrial Revolution, most often to be seen swarming
with tourists. Not that we should be precious about this for
we are all tourists sometime, somewhere. At sunrise the
Iron Bridge briefly stands alone, its integrity uncompromised.
Functional means of crossing the river it may have been but
those of us who lived in the Gorge when tourism was just
an occasional charabanc from the West Midlands were
not wholly ignorant of the origin, importance
and beauty of Darby's masterpiece.

15

Ludlow Castle and River Teme

*T*he castle has physically dominated the town for centuries and for a substantial part of that time exerted a political, economic and social influence. By 1475 it had become the seat of the Council of the Marches, governing Wales and the borders. Castle and town were at a peak of prosperity in the late sixteenth and early seventeenth centuries. The young Philip Sidney, later to become a vaunted poet and courtier, was brought up here, his father Sir Henry Sidney being Lord President of the Marches. Later, John Milton's masque *Comus* had its first performance here in 1634 in honour of the Earl of Bridgwater, a later President. Looking across the peaceful River Teme in the sunlight of the very early morning it does not take too great an imaginative leap to visualise the struggles of power, personality and government which must have taken place here down the years.

Ludlow - River Teme
*L*ooking towards Dinham Bridge with the heights
of the Whitcliffe up to the left.

Long Mynd to Caer Caradoc

A clear night sky with the promise of a spectacular sunrise can quickly turn to photographic anticlimax. On this occasion I got up in what seemed like the middle of the night, rushed down the A49, drove up the deserted Burway and made for my pre-selected viewpoint .... only to discover a claustrophobic canopy of cloud and mist. Cursing my luck and wishing I had stayed in bed I took solace in a flask of coffee. But not all was lost. Within a few minutes a hole in the cloud appeared to let through a few rays of sun which softly illuminated Caer Caradoc.

Long Mynd and the Stretton Hills

*T*aken half an hour after the previous photograph - the rapidly moving cloud and mist rolled away and I was able to shoot a sequence of photographs into the sun as it rose in the sky. The greys and pale yellows, varying in tone, create a natural harmony, like an artist painting with a restricted palette.

Towards Brown Clee

*A*s the sunlight gains in strength the immediate foreground assumes colour and form.

Lyth Hill

A winter sunrise seen from just beyond the garden gate of Spring Cottage, Mary Webb's last home on Lyth Hill.
From here she could see a whole panorama of the hills which were the inspiration for so much of her writing.

The Wrekin

*T*he Wrekin is here seen against a uniform pinkish light,
half an hour or so before sunrise, from Eyton on Severn.
This is Shropshire's best known hill, originally called Mount Gilbert.
For many returning travellers it is a symbol of home. I sincerely hope
that current debates over the future of local government do not
jeopardise what this hill has symbolised for generations
of Shropshire people - unity, not division.

Bishop's Castle

*H*alf past five on an August morning, the sun not yet risen but already
the sky full of colour and the promise of a beautiful day to come.
Beyond the town, this once "rotten borough", rises the bulk
of Corndon Hill just over the border in Wales.

From Bury Ditches

*B*ury Ditches is one of the finest of Shropshire's many Iron Age hillforts. It is situated a few miles south of Bishop's Castle and can be reached from Brockton or Clunton. From the top of its inner ring of ramparts the views are tremendous, perhaps the finest in the county. Coupled with a glorious sunrise they are almost beyond description.

Standing in the middle of this incredible hillfort I watched the sun rise, just as our ancestors would have done from this spot some two thousand years ago. For them, exposed and vulnerable, the warmth and brilliance of the sun must surely have induced a sense of wonder, gratitude and relief.

*I*n the first twenty or thirty minutes after the sun had risen the light changed rapidly,
giving way from brilliance to something more muted and subtle.

Towards The River Kemp

*L*ooking down from Bury Ditches, across Walcot Park, to the valley of the Kemp. The warmth of the day began to draw up a thread of mist from the river. Within a few minutes it was gone.

Morning

O'er nests larks winnow in the wheat,
Till the sun turns gold and gets more high,
And paths are clean and grass gets dry,
And longest shadows pass away.
And brightness is the blaze of day.

(John Clare: from *Morning*)

The Boyne Arms, Burwarton

*T*he minute you arrive in this attractive village you realise that it was, and is, inextricably linked to the estate and the nearby Hall. And as you negotiate the hairpin bends through the village you cannot fail to be impressed by The Boyne Arms (above) with its portico and old stable block, the epitome of a stylish inn of an earlier age.

The Old Church, Burwarton

*S*tanding just a hundred yards or so away from the "new" church (also redundant and now a private residence) are the roofless ruins of Burwarton's original Norman church (top left). I stopped here on a cold, sunny morning in January and enjoyed the atmosphere of gentle tranquility.

A cliche perhaps but the contrast of spring's new growth with evidence of human frailty was one I could not ignore (bottom left).

Abdon Burf

*A*bdon Burf, the actual summit of Brown Clee,
is the highest point in Shropshire at 540 metres.
Extensive quarrying has left a legacy of scars
and dereliction and a somewhat
melancholy atmosphere.

Brown Clee

*L*ooming up out of the stillness of the fog
on a dank autumn morning, this weird example
of communications technology could have come from
a Dr. Who set. Nearby Clee Burf and Titterstone Clee
also have early warning radar systems crowning their
summits. Down below Brown Clee the village of Ditton
Priors once had a military base on its doorstep. During
the Cold War I seem to recall rumours about there being
top-secret goings on here. It was suggested that the
Soviet Union had its missiles trained on Ditton Priors -
a somewhat unlikely theory I would have thought
but a story I have always relished.

Coalmoor

Of Shropshire's many differing landscapes few are as stark as
the constantly shifting open cast mining sites which have
long been such a feature of the district between
Horsehay and Little Wenlock.

Ashford Bowdler

A pretty village, standing between the River Teme and the busy A49. The place is so quiet and secluded that you would never guess there was a trunk road just a couple of hundred yards away. The lovely old church with its shingled tower, more typical of Herefordshire than Shropshire, stands immediately above the river.

A brook, near Shrewsbury

*O*ne of Shropshire's secret places, pictured here
in early February when the snowdrops
literally are a picture.

Atcham: St. Eata's Church

*T*his must be one of the most photographed churches in Shropshire and understandably so for building, trees and river could hardly be more artistically arranged. The hoar frost and slanting rays of sunlight just add to an already picturesque scene.

Near Lea Cross

*W*hile crossing the bridge I noticed these boys messing about in the Rea Brook. Autumn tints and sparkling water completed a timeless scene.

Corbet Wood, Grinshill

*T*he County Council's Countryside Service manages Corbet Woods
where there are delightful walks and easy public access.
On this sunny autumn morning
the colours were superb.

River Severn, Atcham

*"Nobody who has left Shrewsbury by the road...
...forgets the scenery at Atcham. It is four or five miles
out of town, impressive for no grandeur at all,
but for a tranquil beauty pleasant to look back upon
from any day in life. As you cross there the neat
little stone bridge over the Severn, the river below
winds among, and sometimes overflows,
the greenest meadows, here and there
stealing an island out of them."*

(Charles Dickens: from an article
in *All the Year Round*, May 14th 1859)

Long Mynd
from Stiperstones

*I*t never fails to impress me just how a snowfall can transform a familiar scene into something incredibly dramatic. It was certainly true on this occasion when a late snow in April coupled with racing clouds and dazzling sunlight created an apparently new landscape beneath a strange metallic light.

St. Swithin's Church, Cheswardine

*P*arish churches often display wonderful manifestations of medieval carvers'
art in the form of benchends, misericords and those fantastic gargoyles
which look down on mere mortals below. I found this lion at
Cheswardine to be one of the more endearing creations.

Stiperstones

*T*he jagged, frost-shattered outcrops can clearly be
seen in this view from the road near Bridges while
quickly thawing snow highlights the ridges
of fragmented rock on the slopes.

Long Mynd

*T*aken on a misty autumn morning not far from
the village of More. This view shows the impressive
western side of the Mynd, more remote, less
frequented by walkers and tourists than
the batches, hollows and valleys
of the eastern flank.

River Severn near Cross Houses

*Y*ou can almost guarantee that at least once each year, and sometimes two or three times, the Severn will burst its banks and flood low-lying countryside. However many times you have seen it, the sight is still compelling - once again forces of nature transforming a landscape. But spare a thought for the poor souls whose homes are filled with water and silt.

Tern Bridge

A stranger might be forgiven for thinking that this was some wondrous river, of Mississippi proportions. In fact it is the confluence of the Tern and the Severn seen here during winter floods.

Near Cressage

*R*eceding flood waters from the Severn leave sodden fields and rubbish from the river.

On Titterstone Clee

*G*iant "golf balls" like this one are distinctive features of Titterstone Clee like something out of science fiction but actually part of an aviation early warning system. Prior to taking this shot I had spent the two hours since sunrise trying to photographic idyllic rural scenes without aircraft contrails in the sky. It seemed like some plot on behalf of Air Traffic Control to send every available airliner over Shropshire and frustrate my efforts. Perversely, when I got to the summit of Titterstone and actually wanted a contrail in the picture I had to wait half an hour for an aircraft to fly over.

Titterstone Clee

*T*aken from the narrow road up from Dhustone (named after local basalt rock),
the effects of extensive quarrying on the hill can clearly be seen in the photograph.
Quarrying was the major industry in the Clee Hills and, in the latter part of the
nineteenth century and in the years up to the last war, hundreds of men
were employed in this hazardous occupation.

Sundorne Castle

*W*hile investigating the ruinous buildings behind the Sundorne Castle facade I gradually got the feeling that I was being watched. The watcher, amidst these romantic ruins, was no more ghostly than this haughty cat, gazing down at me from his elevated throne.

Sundorne Castle

*N*orth-east of Shrewsbury, just off the B5062, once stood an early nineteenth century brick mansion, built in mock Gothic style. Today little remains apart from a dilapidated chapel, a stretch of castellated wall and this impressive gatehouse which at least gives an indication of the scale and grandeur of the "castle" which was demolished in the late 1950's.

Stretton Hills and Long Mynd

*H*ousman's "blue remembered hills" were the Clees, seen from near his Worcestershire home.
But he is not a topographical poet and we can easily substitute our own mental images.
These are my "blue remembered hills" which always
come to my mind when I read his poem.

St. Mary's Church, Bridgnorth

*B*ridgnorth is a marvellous town for fleeting glimpses, brief snatches of scenes and buildings. Here the dome of this unusual church, designed by Thomas Telford in 1792, can be seen beyond the crazy, leaning ruins of the castle.

Bridgnorth

*T*here can be few towns in Britain more dramatically situated than Bridgnorth. High Town stands along a sandstone ridge, Low Town clusters along the banks of the Severn and an intriguing network of pathways and steps links the two. In this view St. Leonard's Church dominates the skyline while Percy's House (once home of Thomas Percy, editor of the *Reliques of Ancient English Poetry*) faces down river.

44

Granary Steps, Bridgnorth

*O*ne of many ancient flights of steps
in Bridgnorth this one leads down from the lovely
St. Leonard's churchyard, which is so reminiscent
of a cathedral close, to the riverside.

Linley

*T*his simple, unassuming Norman church
stands alongside the drive to Linley Hall,
just off the Broseley to Bridgnorth road.

Green Man

A blocked doorway on the north side of the church has
a carved tympanum featuring a grotesque animal with
human face and branches springing from its mouth.

Kynnersley

*S*tanding near the centre of the little known Weald
Moors is Kynnersley, an attractive village with
cottages and farm buildings clustered
around the church of St. Chad.

The Weald Moors

*A*lthough I have frequently driven across and around the Weald Moors it is only recently that I have stopped, looked more carefully and begun to appreciate the beauty of this rather unusual Shropshire landscape. Here, midway between Preston and Kynnersley, is typical Weald Moor scenery - low-lying, drained land, the road virtually a causeway, and a wide, wide sky.

Crudgington Moor

*T*he Weald Moors were once an extensive area of marshland interspersed with occasional villages sited on slightly higher, firmer ground. These Shropshire fens were drained from the middle of the sixteenth century onwards by a network of ditches and channels. Early in the last century further improvement was undertaken, this time to the roads crossing the area, so benefitting the villages such as Preston, Kynnersley and Eyton.

On Crudgington Moor

*A*t the edge of the woods, alongside the road from Crudgington to Kynnersley,
I noticed this sad little memorial, presumably the gravestone of a beloved
pet belonging to some now long-dead member of the Sutherland family.

Near Cole Mere

*O*vernight snow followed by brilliant sunshine
briefly transforms a pleasant scene
into something rather special.

Cole Mere

With mixed woodland around it on three sides,
glimpses of clear blue water between the trees and
a distant view of Lyneal Church on the fourth, Cole Mere
can be described as a Shropshire gem. Together with
nearby Blake Mere and Bomere Pool near Condover
it was the inspiration for Mary Webb's fictional but
unforgettable Sarn Mere in *Precious Bane*.

Styche Hall

Market Drayton and nearby Moreton Say are inextricably linked with the name of Robert Clive, the legendary Clive of India whose exploits were the very stuff of school history books. With just five hundred men he defeated a French force of ten thousand to ensure British rule in India. He became Governor of India in 1755, won another magnificent military victory at Plassey and later reformed the civil and military services. His life was not without controversy though. A somewhat unruly childhood was followed by hot-headed escapades as a young man and some dubious dealings later on in life which led to opponents in England trying to have him impeached. The House of Commons gave him a vote of confidence but Clive, in poor health now, lived only a few more years before committing suicide in 1774.

The original Styche Hall was Clive's birthplace. The house was rebuilt in the early 1760's by Sir William Chambers, the architect of Somerset House. It is seen here, across fields which Robert would have known, from the village of Longslow.

Market Drayton

*S*ituated right in the north-east corner of Shropshire, almost on the Staffordshire border, Market Drayton deserves to be visited by more people. An hour or two spent in this ancient market town with its buttercross, half-timbered buildings and fine church (whose tower the young Robert Clive reputedly climbed) is well worthwhile. If you can visit on a Wednesday you will discover a marvellous street market - the whole town comes alive as locals and visitors seek out bargains.

Market Drayton now proudly promotes itself as "the home of gingerbread" since it has a centuries old tradition of gingerbread making. It also had an October Damson Fair when the harvest of the many local damson orchards was brought into the town for sale. The fragile blossom of damson trees in one of the surviving orchards is here caught in early sunlight across the River Tern.

Coalport Bridge

*T*wo miles downstream from Ironbridge another
graceful cast-iron bridge was constructed at Coalport
in 1818. The River Severn here can often look deceptively
placid but, with its currents, eddies and whirlpools, it is
a dangerous stretch of water. I have written previously
(in *Shropshire Seasons*) of my rather mixed feelings
about Coalport as it is today. But my early morning walk
around the village and along the river bank to take
this photograph brought back many happy childhood
memories. From our house you could see the bridge and
the river and I was always fascinated, when very young,
as to what lay beyond the intriguing bend just past
the old Gitchfield Brick Works.

Sutton Maddock

St. Mary's was the parish church for our end of Coalport, something like a two mile walk away through woods and across fields.
Not that I speak from experience for the distance was always a good excuse not to attend church on a Sunday. Looking around the churchyard
here on a bitterly cold day in January I was reminded of Thomas Hardy's poem *Friends Beyond* in which he recalls the village worthies he had
known. I too read the gravestones and remembered some of our villagers, people who, when I was a child, were in their prime.
And I remembered some of the stories - of the undertaker who, for a joke one Christmas, had his mates carry him in a new coffin to the
Hundred House at Norton. The landlord somewhat reluctantly agreed to let them bring the coffin in, presumably on the grounds that
it would not be good for business to leave it on view outside. It was duly carried in and placed carefully across a couple of chairs.
As the pints were downed and the evening wore on the coffin lid slowly creaked open, the shrouded "body" rose up and
a deadly hush descended. As I passed his gravestone I could have sworn I heard the words,
"Make mine a pint" issue gently forth on the breeze!

Newport Show

A warm summer morning, animals looking their best, owners and handlers proud of their charges and looking forward to meeting old friends, spectators enjoying themselves - all the makings of a good day out and one that has changed little over the years.

The county's local agricultural shows, Newport, Burwarton, Minsterley, Oswestry and the rest are enjoyable events, part and parcel of Shropshire life. Here (top right) at Newport Show in mid-July Royston Magnus and handler share a contemplative moment.

Three entrants for "Class 93: bull, any age" (bottom right) apparently enjoying titivation prior to judging.

Wappenshall Junction

*I*n the early years of the nineteenth century Wappenshall was an important junction of canals with the tub boat system of the east Shropshire industrial district linking up with the Shrewsbury Canal. A large warehouse was built here, its roof just visible beyond the unusual so-called roving bridge.

Wappenshall

*O*nly a matter of yards from the old warehouse and bridge this short stretch of water is one of the last remnants of the canal. Nature quickly and comprehensively reasserts itself when industrial or commercial activity ceases and a casual passer-by would scarcely visualise what this was like a hundred years or so ago.

Morning

New Works

*T*he north of what is now Telford has by and large changed less than the south. This view over The Rock and Old Park, with Oakengates and Donnington out of sight beyond the ridge, is still typical of the area as I remember it in the 1950's and 1960's. The New Town has brought benefits but it has created problems also and it can be guaranteed to spark off debate and argument whenever the subject is raised. But it is here to stay and I hope that, just as the industrial communities of the eighteenth and nineteenth centuries were an intrinsic part of the wider Shropshire, different but complementary, so Telford will function harmoniously.

Much of the area was in a run down state when the New Town was begun but I do take exception to those who say there was nothing there before Telford. Oakengates, Hadley, Lawley, Trench, St. Georges, Wellington of course, and all the rest were not just names on a map. They were individual communities where generations of people lived and worked. We should respect their individuality, encourage and embrace current changes if they are for the better but never dismiss what went before. Telford is a modern town which has made much of its heritage - Ironbridge, Coalbrookdale and so on. The less glamorous heritage of these other small communities is, to my mind, of equal importance.

Shropshire Union Canal near Market Drayton

*T*he former Birmingham and Liverpool Junction Canal, designed by Thomas Telford, was built to link the two cities but, with the expansion of rail and road transport, was doomed to failure. Today Shropshire's canals are mostly used for recreation, a peaceful canal holiday providing an antidote to the pressures of modern life. This stretch of canal marks the border between Shropshire and Staffordshire and the boat, on this hot July morning, was gently making its way up towards the impressive sequence of locks at Tyrley.

Near More

*T*he cows were clearly in a hurry to get to the farm for milking. I had stopped to photograph the view over the youthful West Onny towards the Long Mynd when, with much snorting, they appeared out of nowhere, piled through the river and headed off across the fields, the farmer trailing behind.

Near Asterton

I was attracted by this view of cattle grazing on a grassy ridge and almost silhouetted against a field of wheat ready for harvesting.

Near Brockton, Bishop's Castle

*I*t was a quarter past six in the morning and there was total silence. I set up my tripod in the farm gateway, confident that nothing would disturb me. I took this one shot and within seconds a landrover roared up the track, prompting a rapid exit on my part and thoughts about Somebody's Law!

Ironbridge Power Station

*A*n early morning view of the cooling towers, concrete and steam harmonising with hazy sunlight,
taken from the low-lying fields alongside the Severn at Buildwas.

Near Buildwas

*T*he Severn Valley Railway used to run below this farmhouse, having followed the river much of the way from Shrewsbury. Buildwas Junction, on the site of the present power station, was the point where the line from Wellington to Much Wenlock crossed the Severn Valley line before winding up the beautiful, tortuous Farley Dingle. Sadly, both lines succumbed to Dr. Beeching.

Uppington

*U*ppington is a pretty village, approached by a tree-lined road off the old A5 from Shrewsbury to Wellington. From the churchyard there are lovely views of the Wrekin and the church itself has considerable interest. In the north wall of the nave is a doorway with a tympanum on which has been carved a crude dragon. This has been dated as eleventh century and Saxon rather than Norman in origin, suggesting that this was originally a Saxon church. However, its history pre-dates even this for in the churchyard, close to the church, is a three foot high fragment of what is thought to have been a Roman altar.

Much Wenlock Priory

*T*he art of topiary, with its stylised and sometimes
fantastic animal shapes, is almost a modern day
perpetuation of medieval stone carving.
These strange creatures, seen very appropriately
against a backdrop of the priory ruins, seem to me
to have much in common with the gargoyles
which adorn many of our churches.

Hampton Loade

One of the so-called "Bewdley Shacks" which were built along the riverside as weekend retreats for West Midlanders, between Bridgnorth and Bewdley. They were home-built, revealing ingenuity of construction, style and decoration. For years they were ignored or belittled by the majority of folk but a few years ago they achieved architectural respectability when they starred in a full length television documentary. This particular bungalow, which stands immediately in front of the Severn Valley railway line, has personal interest for me for it belonged to my great grandparents during the 1920's and early 1930's and they, and other members of the family, would come here regularly for holidays and weekend breaks.

Malvern Hills

On clear days the views from Titterstone Clee are impressive with the Clent and Lickey Hills on the skyline.
A little further round the misty, evocative shapes of the Malverns rise up out of neighbouring Worcestershire.

Afternoon

When light rode high, and the dew was gone,
And noon lay heavy on flower and tree ...

(Percy Bysshe Shelley: from *Twilight*)

Shrawardine

*A*ll that remains of the medieval castle at Shrawardine - a few fragments of stonework and masonry and part of the shell keep, built upon a low, oval mound which was the original Norman motte. The castle survived until the Civil War, latterly belonging to members of the Bromley family who surrendered to the Parliamentarians in June 1645. It was dismantled and much of the stonework used to repair Shrewsbury Castle. This was just one of a chain of small castles running down the western flank of Shropshire, a few miles in from the Welsh border. Once again we see the pull of the west. We still look towards the setting sun but in days gone by people would have looked westwards for other reasons - fear, apprehension, because it was from Wales that, at least in certain periods of history, attack might have come.

River Severn, Shrawardine

*L*ooking out across the Severn and its flood plain towards the Breiddens and Wales.

Near Cleeton St. Mary

*L*ooking north-west towards Brown Clee from the lower slopes of Titterstone Clee. The views from here are tremendous and, on a breezy afternoon such as this one, the place is exhilirating.

In the Clee Hills

*B*etjeman, Clifton-Taylor, Pevsner - all have waxed lyrical about gems of local architechture, sensitive use of local stone, harmony of form and function and so on. But none, to my knowledge, ever expounded on one of Shropshire's art forms - creative use of corrugated iron. Here, on exposed slopes below Titterstone Clee, is a classic example of man's ingenuity and technical sophistication. I say "man's ingenuity" deliberately because I am doubtful as to whether a woman would ever attempt to build such a contraption.

Near Lydham

A typical, unchanging south-west Shropshire scene - farm tucked in the fold of the hills, sheep...
...and more sheep.

Afternoon

Towards Bromlow Callow

A view from Long Mountain, near Brockton, across the valley towards Bromlow Callow. The hill, with its distinctive fringe of trees, is a real landmark, visible from miles away.

Corndon Hill from The Rock

*T*he Rock is the most south-westerly outcrop of the Stiperstones, relatively little known but offering lovely views west to Corndon and further on into Wales.

Heath Mynd

A dramatic combination of brilliant sunshine, illuminating grass and bracken, and a dark, lowering sky.
The farm stands on the division between the lower, cultivated land and the open moors of the hills.

Stream in Winter

*I*cy, fast flowing water and a mossy tree trunk
lurid green in afternoon sunlight.

Tong Church

" *"See - here's the church!"* cried the delighted schoolmaster, in a low voice.
*"And that old building close beside it, is the school-house, I'll be sworn.
Five and thirty pounds a year in this beautiful place!"*

*They admired everything - the old grey porch, the mullioned windows, the
venerable gravestones dotting the green churchyard, the ancient tower, the very
weathercock; the brown thatched roofs of cottage, barn and homestead, peeping
from among the trees; the stream that rippled by the distant watermill; the blue
Welsh mountains far away. It was for such a spot the child had wearied in the
dense, dark, miserable haunts of labour."*

(Charles Dickens: from *The Old Curiosity Shop,* Ch.46)

*D*ickens is known to have stayed in Tong, on Shropshire's eastern border, and his descriptions of church and village match, almost perfectly, what we can still see today. It is a fascinating place, the church filled with the most elaborate tombs and effigies (a verse on one of them often ascribed to Shakespeare). In the novel Little Nell and her grandfather, trying to escape the evil Quilp, take refuge here and enjoy the peace and tranquility which it offers. But Nell, worn out by her troubles, goes into decline. When the novel was first published, in serial form, the whole country held its breath. Would Little Nell recover or would she just fade away? She faded away, in true Victorian fashion. This fictional tragedy led to an early example of the Shropshire tourist industry - Little Nell's "grave" appeared just outside the church porch and for a hundred years or more visitors have stopped to say a prayer for this angelic character. Ignore the author's cynicism here.
Tong Church should be on everyone's itinerary.

Village Fete, Preen Manor

*T*he summer months see a proliferation of posters
advertising village fetes the length and breadth
of the county. I happened upon this one in Church
Preen quite by chance and spent a most enjoyable
afternoon watching and taking part in a variety
of competitions and games of chance.
As always the tombola was a source of earnest
deliberation, while the girl selling raffle tickets for
the more than life-size soft toys
was doing a brisk trade.

*T*here can be few lovelier places to hold a village fete than Preen Manor. The house stands on the site of an old priory and is adjacent to an unusual medieval church which is seventy feet long but only thirteen feet wide. Newly-weds therefore have to walk down the aisle in single file. Preen Manor gardens are open on some afternoons in the summer as part of the National Gardens Scheme. They are among the most beautiful in Shropshire both for their planting and design and for the views, over the terraces, of Wenlock Edge.

Burwarton Show

*T*aking place in early August, a few weeks after
the Newport Show, Burwarton attracts farmers
from Herefordshire and Worcestershire as well
as more local south Shropshire entrants.
Like Newport it has a lovely atmosphere
of serious yet good humoured competition
and a prevailing sense of people
enjoying themselves.

Animals and handlers line up for the judging,
the former, on the whole, more preened
and prettified than the latter.

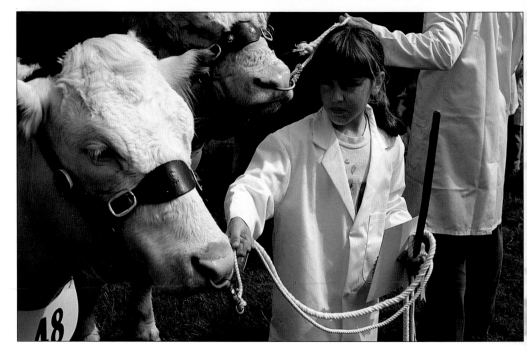

*T*his young lady was clearly in charge as she led
this great beast around the ring. I was thankful
to remain the other side of the rope and make
judicious use of a zoom lens.

*G*etting down to sheep's eye level changes your whole perspective on the Show.

*A*part from the interest of the animals and trade and craft tents I enjoyed just watching other people - the sometimes serious, sometimes lighthearted conversations which struck up between individuals and within groups. Doing a bit of business, having a good gossip is all part of the Show. I hope these gentlemen will excuse me for intruding, albeit discreetly, on their conversations.

Near Harnage

A path through deciduous woods leads to a ruined
cottage, now almost hidden amidst saplings and
undergrowth. In my mind's eye I saw an old fashioned
classroom full of ten year olds seated at wooden desks,
a coke stove at the front of the room and small-paned
windows. And once more I heard those ten year olds
reciting a poem I thought I had forgotten:

Nothing on the grey roof, nothing on the brown,
Only a little greening where the rain drips down;
Nobody at the window, nobody at the door,
Only a little hollow which a foot once wore;
But still I tread on tiptoe, still tiptoe on I go,
Past nettles, porch and weedy well, for oh, I know
A friendless face is peering, and a clear still eye
Peeps closely through the casement
as my step goes by.

(Walter de la Mare: *The Old Stone House*)

84

Beyond the cottage is a clearing with some dilapidated outbuildings and a gate into fields beyond. The scene reminded me of one of those late Victorian paintings, sentimental but nonetheless attractive, of a country scene, the rural idyll. Did the idyll ever really exist?

St. Winifred's Well

*A*nother of Shropshire's discreet treasures. The little half-
timbered cottage is built above the Holy Well of St. Winifred,
a mile or two from West Felton. The saint's body was temporarily
laid to rest here, en route from Holywell to Shrewsbury.
A spring miraculously began to flow and the spot
became a place of pilgrimage.

Near Cound

*T*he breathtaking freshness of newly-emergent leaves
is fleeting - just a week or two in early spring before it fades
and the eye, for so long used to winter colours,
becomes accustomed once again
to many shades of green.

On Hopesay Hill

*L*ooking south-west across the Clun Valley, early on a winter afternoon,
to the remote hills on the Shropshire border.

Near Newcastle on Clun

A typical scene in the south-west corner
of Shropshire - isolated farms, rolling hills,
few trees even though this is known
as Clun Forest. Here you can barely tell
if you are in England or in Wales.

Wart Hill

*T*he delightfully named Wart Hill, seen here from
the bracken covered slopes of Hopesay Hill,
is crowned by banks and ditches of an Iron Age
hillfort, a feature common to so many of the hills
of south and west Shropshire. It is a short,
sharp climb through the trees to the top but
the effort is worthwhile for there are
marvellous views in all directions.

Woods near Harnage

A normally unremarkable view across a recently harvested field is here lifted by the dramatic light.

Hopesay Hill

A green lane on the northern end of Hopesay Hill
with Bury Ditches in the distance.

The Stiperstones

A hot, late August afternoon, a heavy sky and an unusual view of the Stiperstones from the top of Norbury Hill.
From this angle the Stiperstones take on a dome-like aspect which is not apparent when you are walking there.

Linley Hill

*W*ith its instantly recognisable avenue of beech trees Linley Hill is seen from a distance by many people driving along the A488 and A489. Few make the effort to discover one of Shropshire's wonders at first hand. The beeches, reputedly planted in Napoleonic times, have suffered in the gales of recent years. Local people have rallied together and planted dozens of new trees, helping to perpetuate this precious feature for future generations. This photograph shows the top of the avenue and the last pairs of trees - beautiful forms against a wide sky.

Farlow

*E*xploring the villages around the Clee Hills I stopped in the upland village of Farlow and strolled up and down the road in the company of these sheep. They were roaming freely, enjoying the lush grass of the verges and any other vegetation they could reach through garden gates or fences.

On Huglith Hill

*N*ot the normal, friendly welcome one would expect in the Shropshire hills! Having dodged the bullets I was attracted by these vivid hawthorn berries.

Harley

*M*ost counties have their share of unusual place-names but Wigwig and Homer must be up there with the best of them.Writer Philip Turner used them as names for two of his characters in one of his children's books some years ago.

Afternoon

Caer Caradoc

Caer Caradoc is a spectacular hill topped by an impressive hillfort. The Long Mynd and neighbouring hills seem to attract cloud and localise the weather here. Often the hills are rendered even more dramatic when the sun suddenly appears from behind the cloud cover.

Rednal

During the last war the skies over Shropshire were noisy with the sound of aircraft for it was one of the main areas for aircrew training. Airfields were adapted, extended or newly constructed, ranging in size from High Ercall, Shawbury or Atcham down to Montford Bridge, Sleap or Bratton. Today many of them have gone - runways broken up and land returned to farming. But the concrete buildings remain, ruinous eyesore perhaps, but to those with an interest in or memories of those war-time years they are evocative time-warps.

Rednal, near West Felton, was opened in spring 1942 as an OTU (Operational Training Unit) flying Spitfires. The control tower, window frames banging in the breeze, still stands sentinel, looking out over fields. Many of the huts and living quarters of this once extensive airfield are used for light industry - the whine of lathes and saws now breaks the silence which was then filled with the noise of Merlin engines.

My father was stationed here in late 1944 and recalls one of the great fighter pilots of the war, the Canadian George "Screwball" Beurling, undergoing advanced training following what must have been his last tour of duty. Beurling had a reputation as a loner, something of an eccentric who did not take kindly to service discipline. But his gunnery skills were superb and he was credited with destroying at least thirty one enemy aircraft, many of them while defending Malta. Apocryphal stories were told of him - one, that he would walk round the airfield, shotgun in hand, and shoot out any dirty windows which offended his eye. After leaving Rednal he spent the rest of the war as a gunnery instructor but was killed in an air crash in 1948 while ferrying a plane for the Israeli Airforce.

*R*ednal had its share of accidents and fatalities, partly due, no doubt, to the fact that many of the Spitfires were elderly and worn out from combat duty. Again, my father remembers being sent to guard the remains of one which had crashed deep into the ground at Bomere Heath. In 1977 a local aircraft reclamation group recovered the wreckage of another Rednal Spitfire from woodland at The Hincks near Lilleshall. For over thirty years the remains of its Belgian pilot had been buried inside the shattered cockpit. The young man's relatives were located and he was returned to Belgium for burial with full military honours.

The Roveries

*T*he distant trees in this view cover the lower slopes of the hillfort known as The Roveries,
a few miles north of Bishop's Castle and right on the Welsh border.

Afternoon

In the Hope Valley

*T*he road up through the Hope Valley is one of the loveliest in Shropshire and in the autumn
the colours are superb. Mary Webb called this place Dormer Forest:

*Dormer Old House stood amid the remnants of primeval woodland that curtained
the hills. These rose steeply on all sides of the house, which lay low by the water
in the valley. This was called Oolert's Dingle, and there were plenty of owls to
justify the name ...*

(Mary Webb: from *The House in Dormer Forest, Ch.1*)

Celandines

Wood Anemones

Blackthorn Blossom

*I*nto the scented woods we'll go
And see the blackthorn swim in snow ...

(Mary Webb: from *Green Rain*)

Cound Brook

*T*he Cound brook meanders round from Dorrington and Condover,
through Eaton Mascott and Cound to join the Severn opposite Eyton on Severn.
If you are lucky you may just catch sight of a kingfisher,
a flash of turquoise amidst the trees.

Condover Hall

*O*ften acclaimed as the finest Elizabethan house
in Shropshire Condover Hall is now a school for the blind.
It was built for a local judge, Thomas Owen, and is an
impressive sight, its pink sandstone walls contrasting
with the dark green foliage of formal clipped hedges
and bushes . A rather surprising visitor here was the
American writer Mark Twain who visited twice,
at the invitation of Reginald Cholmondeley,
in 1873 and 1879.

Hawkstone Park

*I*n the eighteenth and nineteenth centuries this romantic, exotic parkland was one of the most visited in the country - its rocks and cliffs, follies, caves and ruins were the essential ingredients for the fashionable vogue of the picturesque. The combination of extravagant landscaping on an already dramatic landscape was exploited by successive members of the Hill family. Such was its popularity that what is now the Hawkstone Park Hotel was built to cater for visitors. However, by the end of the last century the family was in financial trouble; the hall was auctioned and the estate split up. The Park went into decline to become a forgotten, decaying but still beautiful shadow of its former state, known only to a few local people.

Afternoon

*I*n 1993, after two years of excavation and renovation, Hawkstone Park was reopened to the public and it is possible
once more to view the splendours which so caught the imagination of Dr. Johnson:

*"... it excells Dovedale, by the extent of its prospects, the awfulness of its shades, the horror of its precipices, the verdure of its hollows
and the loftiness of its rocks. The ideas which it forces upon the mind, are the sublime, the dreadful, and the vast.
Above is inaccessible altitude, below is horrible profundity."*

The Bog

*T*he old mine reservoir, bleak, cold and sombre in the premature gloom of a February afternoon.

Afternoon

Heath Chapel

A near-perfect Norman church, beautiful
in its simplicity, stands alone in a field near
Brown Clee. It was not always so. In the adjoining
field are grassy humps and indentations,
sole reminders of the medieval village
which was once sited here.

Langley Chapel

*L*ike Heath Chapel, Langley stands in a field
a hundred yards or so from the farm which was
once the manor house. The chapel is not as old
as that at Heath, dating from the seventeenth
century, but shares its simplicity
and remote location.

Clun Castle

*T*he massive keep, still imposing in dereliction, and ruins of various towers, are all that remain of the Norman castle which once guarded the vulnerable Clun Valley.

Quatt

*A*fternoon sunlight at Quatt and deep, saturated colours - clear blue sky, lush green and warm red brick.
Quatt is in rich farming country in the south-east of the county. Church and village look westward
across the Severn to Brown Clee and the hills beyond.

Ironbridge Power Station

*T*aken from the new Ironbridge bypass - the massive
cooling towers, their tops level with Benthall Edge,
are now almost part of the natural landscape.

Berrington

A long-locked door is always a small mystery.

From Titterstone Clee

A sombre view out of Shropshire towards
Hay on Wye and the Black Mountains.

Cleobury North

*T*he village is adjacent to the Burwarton
Estate, below Brown Clee, and the church,
Norman in origin, is attractively situated
in a large churchyard amidst trees.

Perkins Beach

*F*rom Stiperstones Village a track leads up a steep-sided valley to emerge on the Stiperstones near
Shepherd's Rock. Ruined cottages and gardens, remnants of mine buildings and ubiquitous
spoil heaps are signs of industry in the valley, long since ceased. The children's writer
Malcolm Saville, popular in the 1950's and 1960's with his Lone Pine adventure stories,
was inspired by the scenery and atmosphere of this district. It became a setting
for several of his books. *Seven White Gates* gives a vivid picture of
the mining dereliction here, much more apparent in the 1940's,
when the book was written, than it is today when so much
has been cleared or reclaimed.

Chirk

*T*he canal aqueduct in the foreground, designed by Thomas Telford, and the railway viaduct beyond span the Ceiriog Valley in spectacular fashion.

Near Eaton Constantine

*I*n the middle of gentle, rolling countryside west of the Wrekin is this solitary chimney and long-defunct kilns of a small brickworks. Shropshire's industry took many and varied forms, often in the most rural locations where natural resources occurred.

Near Rorrington

I had been on Long Mountain on a squally autumn afternoon and decided to drive over towards Bromlow Callow.
As I followed a narrow lane up to Rorrington the sun came out and I just had to take a photograph.

Haughmond Abbey

Shropshire is lucky in having the beautiful ruins of several
substantial monastic buildings - Much Wenlock, Buildwas,
Lilleshall and Haughmond. Here the round arches
of the magnificent chapter house at Haughmond
can be glimpsed through a later doorway.

Shrewsbury, Welsh Bridge

When you are walking in the streets of Shrewsbury, amidst its wealth of buildings dating from medieval times onwards,
it is easy to forget that it is almost encircled by the Severn. The present Welsh Bridge, built by Carline and Tilley in 1795
to replace a medieval structure, leads the traveller westwards out of town and to a choice of routes into Wales -
north-west to Holyhead via the A5, west to Welshpool and mid Wales or south-west to Montgomery or Knighton.
That intriguing western horizon is never far away. I can think of few places better suited than Shrewsbury
to be a county town - geographically central with a varied range of shops and commercial outlets
and with a history and heritage which will stand comparison
with almost any other ancient town in Britain.

Viroconium: the Ermine Street Guard

*B*eing somewhat intrigued by the brown roadsigns proclaiming "Roman Army" which appeared around Atcham and Wroxeter
I decided to find out if this indicated a new invasion of Shropshire, two thousand years on. What it was of course was a demonstration
by the Ermine Street Guard, an authentic recreation of Roman soldiers, marching, training and charging into battle.
And very impressive it was too, particularly with the archaeological remains as a backdrop.

Evening

The day's grown old, the fainting sun
Has but a little way to run.

(Charles Cotton: from *Evening Quatrains*)

Shropshire Union Canal

*Th*e sun breaks through the cloud and is reflected
in the water of the canal which, along this stretch,
runs dead straight above the low lying
peatlands of Whixall Moss.

Belvidere, Shrewsbury

On warm summer evenings starlings settle in their hundreds on this particular pylon,
evidently enjoying their social gathering before nightfall.

Hopton Hills

*N*ewly felled trees with their distinctive scent of bark and resin. I notice that these days timber is no longer felled but "harvested" - well, we do live in the age of the euphemism!

Ellesmere; Shropshire Union Canal

*T*he main traffic on the canal is now leisure craft and in the summer months Ellesmere Wharf is the scene of much coming and going.
Here a boat exits the Wharf to head off past Blake Mere and Cole Mere for Whitchurch. To the right the canal leads to Llangollen
via the spectacular aqueducts at Chirk and Pontcysllte.

Titterstone Clee

And far behind, a fading crest,
Low in the forsaken west
Sank the high-reared head of Clee ...

(A. E. Housman: from *A Shropshire Lad, XXXVII*)

Abdon Burf

*B*rown Clee has twin summits, Clee Burf and Abdon Burf, both heavily quarried in the past.
Abdon Burf is seen here just before sunset above the quarry spoil heaps of its neighbouring summit.

Clee Burf

*T*he Clees have a different atmosphere from the more westerly Shropshire hills. Perhaps it is to do with the abandoned quarries.
Even after activity has ceased the echoes persist.

Nordy Bank

Corvedale and the hill country viewed from yet another
of Shropshire's hillforts, Nordy Bank.

Stokesay Castle

*T*he thirteenth century Great hall and solar range (the living rooms) of Stokesay Castle catch the last light of the sun before it sets behind the hills surrounding the Clun Valley. It is actually a fortified manor house, built by Laurence de Ludlow on the wide valley of the River Onny. The novelist Henry James came here and wrote:

*"I have rarely had .... the sensation of dropping back personally
into the past so straight as while I lay on the grass beside the well
in the little sunny court of this small castle and lazily appreciated
the still definite details of medieval life."*

(Henry James: from *English Hours*)

Breiddens from the Cliffe

*T*he Cliffe is a heath-covered sandstone ridge which extends beyond Nesscliffe and Hopton Hills towards Ruyton-XI-Towns.
From here there is a marvellous view over the Severn and Vyrnwy to the Breiddens.

Devil's Chair, Stiperstones

A declining sun bursts through the gap
in the rocks known as the Needle's Eye.

"A soft, strong wind blew from the west,
quick with the year's promise, brimful of meadow
and mountain scent. Large clouds continually
came up from behind the Chair, darkened it,
swept over the valley, and suddenly
disappeared like conjured ghosts
as the warm air struck them."

(Mary Webb: *The Golden Arrow, Ch. 51*)

131

Stiperstones

*E*arly evening and slanting sunlight leaves the hill above Perkins Beach a dense silhouette.

River Severn, Leighton

A misty, autumn sunset over the Severn, the river just visible between the trees as it meanders
down to Buildwas before entering the Ironbridge Gorge.

Wenlock Edge

*I*n the summer the views from the top of the Edge are frustratingly obscured by trees. Occasionally a gap appears and expectations are rarely disappointed.

River Severn, Atcham

*L*ooking upstream towards Shrewsbury, the sun
about to sink into cloud on the horizon.

White Grit Mine

*T*he ruined engine houses of Shropshire's lead mines are reminiscent of those of the Cornish tin and copper mines. This is no coincidence for these buildings were constructed to house the great Cornish beam engines, used to pump the mines, and many Cornish engineers and miners came up here to join local men in the dangerous ventures. My mother was Cornish and, after Shropshire, I have always considered Cornwall my home from home. I suspect that my affinity with the Stiperstones and the lead mining district round about has something to do with this.

Near Abdon

Snow covered fields above the village of Abdon with a view towards Clun. A less romantic mood came over me when I got back into my car and proceeded to slide down the steep, icy road into the village. Thankfully I managed to negotiate the bends and pass through without leaving my mark on Abdon.

On Nordy Bank

A January sunset behind the hillfort. Local children were still tobogganing down the slopes when I took this and several ponies had come down off the hill, perhaps attracted by the noise and activity or in the hope of food.

Near Melverley

*T*he placid waters of the Severn, near to its confluence with the Vyrnwy, reflecting the last salmon tints of the day.

The Breiddens

A perfect silhouette against the afterglow, taken at ten o'clock on a July evening.

Eyton on Severn

*A*utumn in the Severn Valley. The low lying fields, often flooded in winter, form part of the racecourse for the point to point meetings which are regularly held here.

Berrington

*A*ll Saints' Church stands between trees on the skyline and makes an idyllic sunset scene.

"... Light thickens, and the crow
Makes wing to the rooky wood:
Good things of day begin to droop and drowse,
While night's black agents to their preys do rouse."

(William Shakespeare: *Macbeth: Act III, Scene 2*)

From Nipstone Rock

A marvellously clear evening with views out of Shropshire into Wales from Nipstone Rock on the south-western extension of the Stiperstones.

Mitchell's Fold

*T*here can be few mysteries greater than the stone circles which are to be found across Britain, usually in remote spots -
how or why they were built has never been fully resolved. Mitchell's Fold on Stapeley Hill may not be the largest or most spectacular
of these Bronze Age circles but its location, with views out into Wales (and the setting sun again), is truly impressive.

Wenlock Edge

*T*his was very much a "grab" shot, taken a few years ago before stubble burning was banned. I was driving down towards Hughley at dusk when I happened upon this scene - Wenlock Edge appeared to be on fire. I had no tripod with me and the overall light level was low so I just took the shot and hoped.

Ludlow from the Whitcliffe

*T*his view of Ludlow is probably photographed by hundreds of people each year. But not many, I suspect, take it like this with the lights of church and town in the foreground and a ribbon of streetlights in the far distance at Clee Hill. I would probably not have taken this myself had I not been trying to illustrate a closing passage from one of Sheena Porter's delightful children's books, *Nordy Bank*.

From Haughmond Hill

*T*he last of what had been a magnificent sunset,
looking out over the River Severn and Shrewsbury,
from Haughmond Hill.

Shrewsbury, Lord Hill's Column

A statue of General Viscount Hill tops what is said to be the world's largest Doric column and looks out over the hills of south-west Shropshire and into Wales. Hill, who was born at Prees Hall, had a distinguished military career and served with Wellington in the Penninsula War. Sadly, the statue has fallen into disrepair in recent years and has been removed from the column for extensive repairs. However scaffolding has been re-erected and it seems that the Viscount's return is imminent.

Clun Forest

A hazy sunset near the Shropshire - Welsh border, high in the Clun Forest.

Near Clun

A full, August moon illuminates the hills while the lights of Clun glimmer in the valley below.
Sunrise, sunset, moonrise - the day's cycle is complete.

"... a little river whispered,
full of messages from the west."

(E. M. Forster: from *Howard's End*)

Index of places

A

B

C

E

F

H

I

K

L

More Books on Shropshire published by Shropshire Books:

SHROPSHIRE SEASONS
Gordon Dickins

£14.99

SHROPSHIRE FROM THE AIR
Michael Watson & Chris Musson

£13.99

THE LAND OF LOST CONTENT
Jane Allsopp

£10.99

For a complete list of Shropshire Books titles please write to:

Shropshire Books,
Column House,
7 London Road,
SHREWSBURY,
Shropshire SY2 6NW.